HAL•LEONARD
INSTRUMENTAL
PLAY-ALONG

12 SMASH HITS

MW00784816

THE CD IS PLAYABLE ON ANY CD PLAYER, AND IS ALSO ENHANCED
SO MAC AND PC USERS CAN ADJUST THE RECORDING TO ANY TEMPO
WITHOUT CHANGING THE PITCH!

ISBN 978-1-4803-4124-1

HAL•LEONARD®
CORPORATION
7777 W. BLUEMOUND RD. P.O. BOX 13819 MILWAUKEE, WI 53213

Visit Hal Leonard Online at
www.halleonard.com

CONTENTS

THE A TEAM

1/2

VIOLIN

Words and Music by
ED SHEERAN

GOOD TIME

3/4

VIOLIN

Words and Music by ADAM YOUNG,
MATTHEW THIESSEN and BRIAN LEE

HO HEY

5/6
VIOLIN

Words and Music by JEREMY FRAITES
and WESLEY SCHULTZ

HOME

7/8
VIOLIN

Words and Music by GREG HOLDEN
and DREW PEARSON

I KNEW YOU WERE TROUBLE.

VIOLIN

Words and Music by TAYLOR SWIFT,
SHELLBACK and MAX MARTIN

IT'S TIME

Words and Music by DANIEL REYNOLDS,
BENJAMIN McKEE and DANIEL SERMON

11/12
VIOLIN

LIVE WHILE WE'RE YOUNG

VIOLIN

Words and Music by RAMI YACOUB,
SAVAN KOTECHA and CARL FALK

SKYFALL

from the Motion Picture SKYFALL

15/16
VIOLIN

Words and Music by ADELE ADKINS
and PAUL EPWORTH

TOO CLOSE

VIOLIN

Words and Music by ALEX CLAIRE
and JIM DUGUID

SOME NIGHTS

VIOLIN

Words and Music by JEFF BHASKER,
ANDREW DOST, JACK ANTONOFF
and NATE RUESS

STRONGER
(What Doesn't Kill You)

VIOLIN

Words and Music by GREG KURSTIN,
JORGEN ELOFSSON, DAVID GAMSON
and ALEXANDRA TAMPOSI

WHEN I WAS YOUR MAN

Words and Music by BRUNO MARS,
ARI LEVINE, PHILIP LAWRENCE
and ANDREW WYATT

rit.

Your favorite songs are arranged just for solo instrumentalists with this outstanding series. Each book includes a great full-accompaniment play-along CD so you can sound just like a pro! Check out **www.halleonard.com** to see all the titles available.

Disney Greats

Arabian Nights • Hawaiian Roller Coaster Ride • It's a Small World • Look Through My Eyes • Yo Ho (A Pirate's Life for Me) • and more.

_____	00841934 Flute	$12.95
_____	00841935 Clarinet	$12.95
_____	00841936 Alto Sax	$12.95
_____	00841937 Tenor Sax	$12.95
_____	00841938 Trumpet	$12.95
_____	00841939 Horn	$12.95
_____	00841940 Trombone	$12.95
_____	00841941 Violin	$12.95
_____	00841942 Viola	$12.95
_____	00841943 Cello	$12.95
_____	00842078 Oboe	$12.95

Glee

And I Am Telling You I'm Not Going • Defying Gravity • Don't Stop Believin' • Keep Holding On • Lean on Me • No Air • Sweet Caroline • True Colors • and more.

_____	00842479 Flute	$12.99
_____	00842480 Clarinet	$12.99
_____	00842481 Alto Sax	$12.99
_____	00842482 Tenor Sax	$12.99
_____	00842483 Trumpet	$12.99
_____	00842484 Horn	$12.99
_____	00842485 Trombone	$12.99
_____	00842486 Violin	$12.99
_____	00842487 Viola	$12.99
_____	00842488 Cello	$12.99

Motown Classics

ABC • Endless Love • I Just Called to Say I Love You • My Girl • The Tracks of My Tears • What's Going On • You've Really Got a Hold on Me • and more.

_____	00842572 Flute	$12.99
_____	00842573 Clarinet	$12.99
_____	00842574 Alto Saxophone	$12.99
_____	00842575 Tenor Saxophone	$12.99
_____	00842576 Trumpet	$12.99
_____	00842577 Horn	$12.99
_____	00842578 Trombone	$12.99
_____	00842579 Violin	$12.99
_____	00842580 Viola	$12.99
_____	00842581 Cello	$12.99

Popular Hits

Breakeven • Fireflies • Halo • Hey, Soul Sister • I Gotta Feeling • I'm Yours • Need You Now • Poker Face • Viva La Vida • You Belong with Me • and more.

_____	00842511 Flute	$12.99
_____	00842512 Clarinet	$12.99
_____	00842513 Alto Sax	$12.99
_____	00842514 Tenor Sax	$12.99
_____	00842515 Trumpet	$12.99
_____	00842516 Horn	$12.99
_____	00842517 Trombone	$12.99
_____	00842518 Violin	$12.99
_____	00842519 Viola	$12.99
_____	00842520 Cello	$12.99

Sports Rock

Another One Bites the Dust • Centerfold • Crazy Train • Get Down Tonight • Let's Get It Started • Shout • The Way You Move • and more.

_____	00842326 Flute	$12.99
_____	00842327 Clarinet	$12.99
_____	00842328 Alto Sax	$12.99
_____	00842329 Tenor Sax	$12.99
_____	00842330 Trumpet	$12.99
_____	00842331 Horn	$12.99
_____	00842332 Trombone	$12.99
_____	00842333 Violin	$12.99
_____	00842334 Viola	$12.99
_____	00842335 Cello	$12.99

Women of Pop

Bad Romance • Jar of Hearts • Mean • My Life Would Suck Without You • Our Song • Rolling in the Deep • Single Ladies (Put a Ring on It) • Teenage Dream • and more.

_____	00842650 Flute	$12.99
_____	00842651 Clarinet	$12.99
_____	00842652 Alto Sax	$12.99
_____	00842653 Tenor Sax	$12.99
_____	00842654 Trumpet	$12.99
_____	00842655 Horn	$12.99
_____	00842656 Trombone	$12.99
_____	00842657 Violin	$12.99
_____	00842658 Viola	$12.99
_____	00842659 Cello	$12.99

Twilight

Bella's Lullaby • Decode • Eyes on Fire • Full Moon • Go All the Way (Into the Twilight) • Leave Out All the Rest • Spotlight (Twilight Remix) • Supermassive Black Hole • Tremble for My Beloved.

_____	00842406 Flute	$12.99
_____	00842407 Clarinet	$12.99
_____	00842408 Alto Sax	$12.99
_____	00842409 Tenor Sax	$12.99
_____	00842410 Trumpet	$12.99
_____	00842411 Horn	$12.99
_____	00842412 Trombone	$12.99
_____	00842413 Violin	$12.99
_____	00842414 Viola	$12.99
_____	00842415 Cello	$12.99

Twilight – New Moon

Almost a Kiss • Dreamcatcher • Edward Leaves • I Need You • Memories of Edward • New Moon • Possibility • Roslyn • Satellite Heart • and more.

_____	00842458 Flute	$12.99
_____	00842459 Clarinet	$12.99
_____	00842460 Alto Sax	$12.99
_____	00842461 Tenor Sax	$12.99
_____	00842462 Trumpet	$12.99
_____	00842463 Horn	$12.99
_____	00842464 Trombone	$12.99
_____	00842465 Violin	$12.99
_____	00842466 Viola	$12.99
_____	00842467 Cello	$12.99

Wicked

As Long As You're Mine • Dancing Through Life • Defying Gravity • For Good • I'm Not That Girl • Popular • The Wizard and I • and more.

_____	00842236 Book/CD Pack	$11.95
_____	00842237 Book/CD Pack	$11.95
_____	00842238 Alto Saxophone	$11.95
_____	00842239 Tenor Saxophone	$11.95
_____	00842240 Trumpet	$11.95
_____	00842241 Horn	$11.95
_____	00842242 Trombone	$11.95
_____	00842243 Violin	$11.95
_____	00842244 Viola	$11.95
_____	00842245 Cello	$11.95

FOR MORE INFORMATION, SEE YOUR LOCAL MUSIC DEALER, OR WRITE TO:

HAL•LEONARD® CORPORATION

7777 W. BLUEMOUND RD. P.O. BOX 13819 MILWAUKEE, WI 53213